100 Things to
Always Remember...
and One Thing
to Never Forget

Blue Mountain Press ®

Boulder, Colorado

100 Things to
Always Remember...
and One Thing
to Never Forget

by Alin Austin

Library of Congress Catalog Card Number: 93-25766
ISBN: 0-88396-373-6

Acknowledgments: This book was written by
Douglas Richard Pagels. It is dedicated
to friends and family members, in whose
company I have received many reminders of
the joy to be found in simple wisdom. And
it is dedicated to my two sons and my wife,
who continually teach me the wisdom to be
found in simple joys.

n *design on book cover is registered in*
U.S. Patent and Trademark Office.

Manufactured in the United States of America
First Printing: August, 1993

Library of Congress Cataloging-in-Publication Data

Austin, Alin, 1950-
    100 things to always remember — and one thing to never forget / by
Alin Austin.
        p.   cm.
    ISBN 0-88396-373-6
    1. Conduct of life.   2. Success.   I. Title.   II. Title: One
hundred things to always remember — and one thing to never forget.
BJ1581.2.A87   1993
170'. 44—dc20   *93-25766*
                                                          CIP

This book is printed on fine quality, laid embossed, 80 lb. paper. This paper has been
specially produced to be acid free (neutral pH) and contains no groundwood or
unbleached pulp. It conforms with all of the requirements of the American National
Standards Institute, Inc., so as to ensure that this book will last and be enjoyed by
future generations.

Blue Mountain Press ®

P.O. Box 4549, Boulder, Colorado 80306

CONTENTS

Remember

Your presence is a
present to the world.
You're unique and one
of a kind. Your life
can be what you want
it to be. Take the days
just one at a time.

Remember

*C*ount your blessings,
not your troubles.
You'll make it through
whatever comes along.
Within you are so many
answers. Understand,
have courage, be strong.

Don't put limits on yourself. So many dreams are waiting to be realized. Decisions are too important to leave to chance. Reach for your peak, your goal, your prize.

Remember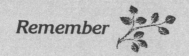

Nothing wastes more energy than worrying. The longer one carries a problem, the heavier it gets. Don't take things too seriously. Live a life of serenity, not a life of regrets.

Remember

*Think about getting rich:
friendships are priceless,
time is invaluable, health
is wealth, and love is a
treasure. Have a nest egg
of beautiful memories that
you can dip into from time
to time to ease any sorrows.
Have the kind of remembrances
that raise you up with their
worth and keep you there
with their wonder. And have
a secret supply of hopes on
hand to help you plan
your tomorrows.*

Share your good fortune with the people who are at the center of the circle of your life. If you invest in your dreams, it's impossible to overpay. Give away smiles, and watch them come back to you a hundred times over. Spend your twenty-four hours wisely and well each day.

Stuff your pockets with kindness and optimism; there is nothing more precious in the world. It's really kind of funny: Someday, you'll look back on your life, and you'll realize that the riches you prized . . . had absolutely nothing to do with money.

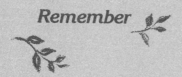
*L**et the children be happy.
Teach them to fill their hearts
with feelings of wonder and to
be full of courage and hope.
Nothing is more important than
the sharing of this moment in
time. Hold their kite strings,
make their hearts sing, make
their smiles shine.*

*Reflect their inner and outer
beauty. Encourage them to be
in less of a hurry. Show them
that you have the patience of a
saint, and try to have the
understanding of one, too.
Admire them. Inspire them.
And tell them in untold ways
what they mean to you.*

Remember

If you sometimes feel
like you don't fit in,
join the club. Don't keep
your inner voice silent;
let yourself hear it. Be
on good terms with the
person who lives inside
of you. It doesn't cost
anything to be a free spirit.

If your self-esteem falls overboard, throw out a rescue line. Pull yourself back together, wherever you're at. Don't be your own worst critic; be your own best ally. Because you're worth it, that's why.

And that's that.

Remember

*S*ometimes it's important to
work for that pot of gold.
But other times it's essential
to take time off and to make
sure that your most important
decision in the day simply
consists of choosing which
color to slide down on the
rainbow.

Remember

Many of us have roadmaps
we envision for the courses we
think our lives should take.
It's important to get headed
in the right direction, but
don't get so caught up in the
concerns over your destination
that you forget to delight in
the scenery of each new day.
Remember that some of the
secret joys of living are not
found by rushing from point A
to point B, but by inventing
some imaginary letters
along the way.

This is a magnificent journey you're on. Don't be afraid to explore unfamiliar territory. If you do happen to get lost, you will stumble across some of the most interesting discoveries you will ever make. Wander down roads you've never taken before or ones you'll never chance upon again. Life isn't a travel guide to follow. It's an adventure to undertake.

Remember

*B*e creative.
You're the artist here.
You're the one who can
brush away the clouds
and make the sun shine.
Paint your own picture,
choose your own colors.
And forget all that
business about having to
stay between the lines.

Find the pace of life
that works best for you.
Always marching to someone
else's beat is like living
a charade. Don't be too
bored with one pace, or too
overextended with another.
Get in step with your
own parade.

You're an original, an individual, a masterpiece. Celebrate that; don't let your uniqueness make you shy. Don't be someone other than the wonder you are. Every star is important to the sky.

Remember

Do your part for the planet.
Do all the things you know you
"should" do. Our grandchildren's
children will either have words
of praise for our efforts and our
foresight, or words that condemn
us for forgetting that they must
live here long after we are gone.
Don't overlook the obvious:
This is not a dress rehearsal.
This is the real thing. Our
presence has an impact, but our
precautions do, too. And the
environment means the world to us.

Remember

Greet the day with an enthusiastic welcome. Just watch . . . and it will respond accordingly. Acknowledge that sure, some things may be impossible. But you'll have to take it to the limit to see.

The darkest hour is the best time to see the stars. Keep your spirits up; you'll find that optimism is very refreshing. The wisest people on earth are those who have a hard time recalling their worries . . . and an easy time remembering their blessings.

Remember

*T*ime can't take away
anything that has already been
given: Your treasures from days
gone by are treasures still; your
most precious memories will
always be. We learn, as we
go along, that life is not
one big, beautiful jewel we
can hold — or lose — in our
hands. Each one of us is an
hourglass. And in the course
of our lives, we get to keep
the diamonds that come our way
among the passing sands.

Remember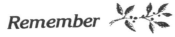

*If you're going to do it,
do it like you mean it.
Just realize that it
can be good or bad to go
to the extreme. If you're
willing to risk it all,
maybe you can have it all.
But you'd better make sure
you're dreaming the right dream.*

Don't give up. You may not know success if you stop trying one attempt too soon. Try to get better in some way, each and every day. They say that room for improvement is always our biggest room.

Remember

*F*ollow your hopes and dreams
while you can. While the desire
is burning. When the chance
comes your way. Don't be a
ship that stays in the harbor,
never straying from its safety.
Don't get tangled up with
"maybe . . . maybe someday."
Too many folks will tell you
that if you spend your whole
life waiting, "someday" arrives
too little, too late. Maybe
it's already a little later
than it seems. If you really
want to do it, do it while you
can. Be brave . . . and sail away
on your dreams.

Unlike any other creature on earth, we alone are capable of imagining the worst. Rather than simply dealing with reality, we can create mountains impossible to cross. That's no way to go through life! Those who think that "Murphy's Law" is the governing rule are always going to find themselves at a loss.

Don't take troubles — yours or those of the world — to sleep with you. Pay attention to the news, but don't pay homage to it. When they're taken all together, problems have a contagious way of compounding. Find a way to turn off the day. Make sure you have a private place where you can get away from it all — a sanctuary in the midst of your surroundings.

Remember

Don't feel like you have to choose between traditional choices. Whether to be a big fish in a little pond or a little fish in a big pond may not have an ounce of relevance to what your spirit wants to do. Maybe you need to be a speckled trout in a wilderness river or a flying fish in a tropical sea. Pigeonholes are for pigeons . . . not for people like you.

Remember

If your pursuit of wealth causes you to sacrifice any aspect of your health, your priorities are turned around. Your physical condition is your compass; it will tell you if you are headed in the right direction or if you're going astray. It's not your checkbook, but <u>you</u> who is counted on to be there for the people in your world. Be far-sighted. Weigh the differences. Think of the prices to pay.

Resist the urge to take anything for granted. Changes always come along, some for the better, some for the worse. The people who manage to make it through the turns in the road understand this, and they take their place in the driver's seat, headed for tomorrow, secure in the knowledge that nothing is more natural than change. And the natural way is the only way it works.

Remember

The best way to handle
the future is to be like
a carpenter on a job.
First, make sure the work
on the foundation is all
through. Then, just show
up on time, bring along all
the tools you'll need, and
keep a level head about you.

Remember

Share your magic with the people who share your memories. Have feelings that run very deep. Be in touch with the people who live in your heart. Be a caring person who plays for keeps.

*T*he secret of life is to
make the best of whatever
comes along. Make every day
fresh and new. Go in search
of knowledge and experience.
Let your questions and your
answers reconcile. And do
your best to remember . . .

The best kind of learning
curve is an educated smile.

Remember

*T*o really know what success
means, earn it. Don't rely on
some elevator to get you there.
The easiest lessons to
remember are the ones you
learn the hard way. The
higher the floor you want
to reach, the more important
it is to take the stairs.

Remember

*O*ne of the injustices of life
is being judged by others,
when those judges might be
guilty, too. Don't scrutinize
people with a microscope;
view them from a comfortable
distance. And allow some room
for compassion in the space
that lies between you.

*Everyone has an agenda.
Maybe it will help if you
remember that. To better
understand a person involves
being aware of the depth of
their needs. People are like
clocks. And here's the
interesting part of it:
You can look them in the face
and get an idea of what's
going on at the time, but the
essential thing is figuring
out what makes them tick.*

Remember

*G*o out of your way to be good to an older person. You'll discover that you can make somebody's entire day with a smile, a phone call, some fresh-picked daisies, or whatever it is you've got.

Our elders have so much to give to those who listen, but they are the ones who deserve to receive. Don't pass up the chance to brighten their lives. An old adage reminds us that they need only a little, but they need that little — a lot.

Remember

If you're hurting, get on the path to healing. Feel comfortable with inevitable moments of doubt. Build on your past strength and move towards your highest hopes. The answers are there to search for and seek out.

You'll figure out what to do when difficulties arise. Problems come and go as naturally as the seasons. One solution to remember is that it can sometimes be better to do the wrong thing for the right cause — than the right thing for the wrong reason.

In the story of your life, write the best book you can. Have pages on understanding and tales of overcoming hardships. Fill your story with romance, adventure, poetry, and laughter. Make each chapter reflect time well spent. Meet your obligations, but take time to greet your aspirations. If you live up to your potential, you'll never have to live down any disappointment.

Remember

Don't let life's opportunities slip through your fingers. There are so many challenges you can find. There are so many goals worth fighting for. One of the best is peace of mind.

There *are choices ahead*
which could change your
life. Unfortunately, no
crystal ball has any
forecast to impart. But
centuries of wisdom have
never improved on the advice:
Just listen . . . to your heart.

*A*dmire your accomplishments.
Large or small, tremendous
or tiny, they contribute
to the well-being of this
world. A little light
somewhere makes a brighter
light everywhere. A speck
of sand can turn into a pearl.

Remember

Enjoy the questions as much as the answers. Offset what's wrong by making twice as many things right. Don't insist on everything being predictable. Life is full of surprises, and surprises are full of life.

Remember that a little love goes a long way. Remember that a lot . . . goes forever. Remember that friendship is a wise investment. Life's treasures are people . . . together.

Remember

*R*ealize that it's never
too late. Do ordinary
things in an extra-
ordinary way. Have
health and hope and
happiness. Take the
time to wish upon a star.

*A*nd don't ever forget
— for even a day —
how very
special
you are.